LIVE LIKE A

HUNTER GATHERER

DISCOVERING THE SECRETS OF THE STONE AGE

NAOMI WALMSLEY

ILLUSTRATED BY
MIA UNDERWOOD

Button
BOOKS

CONTENTS

WHAT WAS THE STONE AGE?

The Stone Age was the start of all human history, spanning about three million years. Human species evolved, tools were made from stone and bone, people hunted and foraged for food and wore clothes made from animal skins. Early humans had to work hard to survive and thrive.

Myth busting

What do you think of when you imagine the Stone Age? Here are some common myths:

Early humans weren't very clever

Actually, they needed to know everything about their environment, the animals, the weather, where to find food, hunting techniques, making tools and endless other things. They were probably some of the wisest people that have ever lived.

They said 'ugg' all the time

Homo sapiens have probably been using complex language for at least 200,000 years. For early hominids, whose speech hadn't yet developed, they may have had smart ways to communicate using actions, grunts, clicks and drawing on walls.

They lived alongside dinosaurs

Dinosaurs were a resilient bunch and lasted about 165 million years on Earth but, luckily for our ancestors, they were wiped out about 65 million years ago.

A Stone Age friend

I would love to show you a bit about my world. I have seen eight summers so far. I live, sleep, play and eat with my ma and pa and the rest of my tribe. Sometimes we live in rock shelters with a cosy fire, at other times my blanket is just the stars above my head and my light is the moon. I want to share wild hunting stories with you, tell you about the beasts that roam the land with me and about my favourite foods. My past has carved out your future. Come with me on this journey and we'll share some Stone Age secrets.

Nowadays, we have central heating, houses to live in, supermarkets full of food and water in the tap. So easy!

Early human evolution

A 'human' is anyone who belongs to the genus *Homo* (Latin for 'man'). Scientists still don't know exactly when or how the first humans evolved but they've identified a few of the oldest types.

The first human family began in Africa but other close relations also appeared later on other continents, such as Asia and Europe. They had names like *Homo habilis*, *Homo ergaster*, *Homo erectus* and, us modern humans, *Homo sapiens* (there were many more).

Hominids

The word 'hominid' describes the members of the biological family called *Hominidae*. This includes humans, gorillas, chimpanzees and orangutans. It includes species that are alive today and ones that are extinct.

But wait... there wasn't just one species of human, there were many! One of these was a species called Neanderthals. Think of them like a distant cousin. They existed about 100,000 years before *Homo sapiens* but became extinct about 30,000 years ago.

Humans that look and behave a bit more like you and me did not exist until about one million years ago.

Homo neanderthalensis

Homo habilis   Homo ergaster   Homo erectus   Neanderthal   Homo sapiens

MAPPING THE STONE AGE

The first early humans, like *Homo ergaster*, *Homo erectus* and *Homo sapiens* emerged in Africa around two million years ago, but they didn't all stay there. Scientists are still trying to figure out exactly when and why they began to move. Perhaps it was because of a change in climate, to find food or maybe they didn't get on with their neighbours?

Wolverine

Arctic fox

Skara Brae (Scotland)
Neolithic settlement

Mastodon

Wild horse

Giant beaver

NORTH AMERICA

Stonehenge (England)
Neolithic standing stones

Meadowcroft Rockshelter (USA)
North America's oldest known human settlement

Sabre-tooth tiger

Lascaux cave (France)
Upper Paleolithic cave paintings

Cave hyenas

AFRICA

Mesa Verde (USA)
Ancient cliff dwellings

Aurochs

***Homo sapiens* were one of the last types of early human to leave Africa, joining many other species of early humans already living in other parts of the world. In Europe, they lived alongside Neanderthals for at least 5,000 years.**

Cerro Azul rock art (Colombia)
12,000 years old

SOUTH AMERICA

The first *Homo sapiens* migrated to the Americas about 20,000 years ago.

Blombos cave (South Africa)
Oldest known drawing by *Homo sapiens* found on a rock fragment

Cueva de las Manos (Argentina) Large areas of cave art

The word 'megafauna' means 'big animal'. Many of the animals in the Stone Age were much larger than the ones we share our Earth with today.

Dolni Vĕstonice (Czech Republic) Venus figurine found here, 26,000 years old

Sunghir burials (Russia) Upper Paleolithic burial site, 13,000 ivory beads found in the graves

Woolly mammoth

ASIA

Giant deer

Cave bears

Cave lion

Woolly rhinoceros

EUROPE

The first *Homo sapiens* migrated into Europe about 40,000 years ago.

Denisova cave (Siberia) Remains found of ancient horse species

DNA from an unknown species of early human was found in the Denisova cave in 2010. They are now known as 'Denisovans'.

The first *Homo sapiens* migrated into Asia about 200,000 years ago.

Göbekli Tepe (Turkey) Neolithic place of worship

The first *Homo sapiens* migrated into Australia about 60,000 years ago.

Madjedbebe (Australia) Sandstone rock shelter, oldest evidence of humans in Australia

Afar region (Ethiopia) Remains of early hominid skeletons found here: 'Lucy' (3.2 million years old) and 'Ardi' (4.4 million years old)

Giant wombat

AUSTRALIA

The earliest known hominids lived in Africa around six million years ago.

Giant kangaroo

Giant goanna

TIMELINE OF THE STONE AGE

Three main time periods help break up the Stone Age into sections, showing the changes over time and the discovery of new skills and ways of living. It all started with the **Paleolithic** (old Stone Age), continued into the **Mesolithic** (middle Stone Age) and ended after the **Neolithic** (new Stone Age).

Lower Paleolithic
3 million years ago (2,800,000 BCE)

Early forms of humans roamed the land

Basic stone and bone tools were used

Flint knapping began (shaping with hammer stones)

Clothing was very basic

People survived by scavenging

Middle Paleolithic
300,000 years ago (298,000 BCE)

Homo sapiens started to appear in Africa

People hunted in small groups

Ways to make fire were discovered

Hand axes were used

Lower Paleolithic

Middle Paleolithic

Upper Paleolithic

Upper Paleolithic
40,000 years ago (38,000 BCE)

Homo sapiens begin to appear in Europe

People began living in rock shelters

Bone tools became more sophisticated

About one third of the Earth was covered in ice

Spear throwers began to be used

Cave art showing animals and hand prints was created

People began hafting their tools (attaching points and creating handles)

Evidence found for first boats made from logs

Travelling across continents was now easier

Bows and arrows were used

People hunted and gathered in warmer, wetter lands, like forests

Mesolithic
10,000 years ago
(8,000 BCE)

About 20,000 years ago *Homo sapiens* spread to North and South America

Mesolithic

Mesolithic

Neolithic

Neolithic
8,000–3,000 years ago,
(6,000–2,000 BCE)

Stonehenge was built in the late Neolithic

Farming began, growing grains, fruits and nuts, cultivating the land using ploughs made from antler and wood

People began to domesticate local wild animals like wild boar and aurochs

Clay pots were being made

People lived in larger communities and towns

Permanent homes were built

STARTING A FIRE

One of the most important discoveries ever made was how to make and control fire. Our ancestors would have been intrigued by flames and found ways to use existing fires for their gain, but learning how to make fire from nothing didn't happen until about 300,000 years ago.

Rock banging

Banging two rocks together to create a spark is a technique that early humans may have used.

Friction

Embers were also created by friction using sticks and a piece of hearth wood. The fine wood dust is heated up, producing a hot ember.

From spark to flames

Using a natural tinder, such as dried fungus, roughed-up birch bark, dried grasses and leaves, a spark would have been delicately transferred and, with a tender blow of air, turned into flames.

Carrying fire

It was useful to be able to carry an ember to be awakened when arriving at a new place. By making a tight bundle from dry grasses and leaves inside a flexible piece of bark, tied up with natural cordage or roots, our ancestors would have been able to carry a smouldering ember for hours.

MAKE A SPARK

Today, we have lighters and matches to start fires, but do you think you could make a spark the Stone Age way? Have a go at this activity and you will find out that it isn't as easy as it looks.

You will need

- **A piece of flint** (with a sharp edge)

- **A high-carbon steel** striker with an edge or ferrocerium rod (these can be bought from outdoor shops or found online)

- **You can also use** old metal woodworking files or, for a more authentic approach, you can try a piece of marcasite (but it can be hard to get hold of and takes a lot of practice)

A piece of flint (with a sharp edge)

Take the piece of flint in your left hand (if you are right-handed) and strike the steel down against it as if you were trying to shave off a small piece of the edge of the steel. Watch for any sparks produced and keep practising!

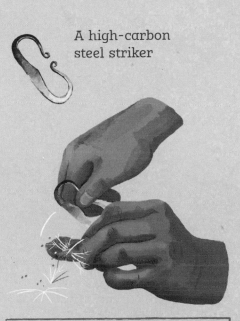

A high-carbon steel striker

Let an adult know what you are doing and practise this activity in a safe place.

Big changes

Fire changed human evolution. People could be warm and have light, so their day could be much longer. It meant protection from wild animals and being able to cook food. Once our ancestors started cooking meat, their food was more easily digested, making it safer to eat and easier to chew. Their brains grew with the extra nourishment and less chewing meant more time to chat, allowing for language and group activities to develop.

TYPES OF SHELTER

Just like us modern folk, early humans needed shelter to survive. Having a shelter or not could have meant the difference between life and death, by offering shade from the sun, a covering from the rain, a barrier from the wind and protection from wild beasts.

Paleolithic shelters

Our earliest ancestors have the reputation of being cave dwellers. But was this really the case? Caves can't be built and were quite rare to find. How many caves have you seen recently? Exactly! Caves are dark, dank and stinky and, without a chimney, it would have been a smoky place to have a fire. More likely, our ancestors would have found rock shelters. Imagine an over-hanging rocky ledge creating a roof. Sling up an animal hide or two for a doorway and this would have made a great place to hang out for a while.

Can you imagine being sent inside a cave to check for sleeping cave bears or hungry sabre-tooth tigers?

Mesolithic shelters

With the ice having melted in the Mesolithic era, people were free to move around, to find food and lush lands. Tribes would have moved with the seasons and the migrating animals, so temporary structures would have been built, like small huts and tepee-style shelters. These huts would be light and easy to move around, made of a wooden frame and covered with animal skin, grass or perhaps tree bark and large leaves.

Neolithic shelters

During these times, people started settling in the same place. They had begun farming and living in small communities, so people began building more permanent homes. This would have involved building a structure from sticks, weaving around grasses and reeds and then filling in the gaps with a mix of soil, clay, animal dung, dried wheat and grasses. This is called daub (see below) and creates a warm and watertight covering when dried. The roofs were thatched with straw (from wheat). It worked so well that some homes today are still made using these techniques.

It can be hard work building a shelter, even if it's just temporary, so everyone would have played a part in helping to set up camp.

Inside a Neolithic shelter

Have you ever made a shelter outside? You can find instructions on how to build a Mesolithic hideout on page 14.

Mucky work!

To mix the sticky daub mixture for house building, tribes may have used their hands, sticks or perhaps they got the cattle involved by stomping over it? They may even have mashed it up with their bare feet. Can you imagine squidging around barefoot in animal poo and clay?

BUILD A MESOLITHIC SHELTER

The best place to make this simple Mesolithic shelter is in a woodland, where nature offers you the materials you need, right there on the ground. Remember to get permission if you want to sleep in it and leave nothing behind when you leave.

You will need

- **1 ridge pole** about as tall as you with your arms stretched out above your head and about as thick as your wrist

- **2 Y-shaped door frame poles** that reach from the ground to your belly button, no thicker than your wrist

- **Lots of sticks** of varying lengths to fill in the gaps

- **Leaf litter** and twiggy branches for covering

- **Length of string** or rope (optional)

1 Lean the two Y-shaped sticks inwards towards one another so that they link and hold together to form a triangle.

2 Balance the long ridge pole at the top of the triangle and rest the other end on the ground. This should stand alone once you let go but you can lash it together with a bit of string or rope if you like.

3 Lay sticks along both sides, making sure there is enough space inside the shelter for you to lie down. It will start to look a bit like a rib cage. Each stick should have its place, smaller ones at the bottom and bigger ones at the top. Keep the doorway clear. Cover the frame with a final layer of leaves and twiggy branches, from the bottom upwards.

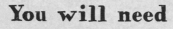

If you want to sleep in your shelter, it will need a thick covering of leaves or a tarp thrown over the top. Our ancestors would have used a few animal skins for this.

MAKE A FAT LAMP

Our early ancestors relied on light to be able to craft, cook and create cave art. They could have used shells or rocks for their lamps, the fat from animals, plants and seeds, and a wick made from natural plant fibres, mosses or grasses.

You will need

1

- **A ball of air-dry clay** about the size of a ping-pong ball
- **Some fat**, which could be lard, coconut oil, olive or sunflower oil
- **Natural garden twine** the length of your thumb
- **Matches** or a lighter (ask an adult to help you when using these)

2

1 Push your thumb into the centre of the ball of clay to make an indent. Using your thumb and index finger, pinch the sides all the way around evenly. The walls should be about ⅜in (1cm) thick.

2 Gently pinch a spout shape in one section. This is where the wick will sit.

3 Fill the lamp with your chosen oil. Place the twine in and carefully light it.

Nut Lamps

Nuts and seeds can be full of useful oils. Why don't you see if you can use them to create a natural lamp? Walnuts, pecans and Brazil nuts work well. Grind up about three nuts with a hard stone on a board until they make a paste. Gather it all up to make a little pyramid shape and then light the top.

3

SLEEPING IN A ROCK SHELTER

It is time to move camp. The leaves are starting to brown and each day the sun leaves the sky quicker, giving way to the eager light of the moon. The animals are making their journeys to warmer lands and Pa says we should follow them. I roll up my reindeer sleep mat, deer-skin blanket, slingshot, fish-skin pouch full of dried berries and nuts, and my little clay pots. We thank our camp for the shelter and protection it has given us and set off with our tribe, hoping to find somewhere safe to camp, for as long as the sun can safely guide us on our journey.

Just as the sun is getting tired and dipping behind the mountains one of the elders called out from ahead that they've found a rock shelter. It is on a slope, but looks like there is enough flat ground to hold us all in sleep. I am relieved it isn't a deep cave. Deep caves are cold and have a peculiar thick wet type of smell that belongs to no one and you just never know what might lurk in the dark bits.

We have to work quickly, using the last of the sunlight to collect wood and awaken a fire. Ma produces a handful of dried bark from her leather pouch and we all work together turning the wood in its hearth, making it spin round and round, eventually releasing the hidden heat, a delicate ember. We tenderly blow and then we have the precious fire.

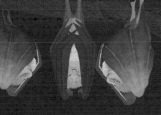

Our peace is shattered as a thick, chattering black swirl echoes high-pitched squeals over our heads, alarming our tribe. We have awakened bats with our smoke, too many to count. A cloud of confused tiny black monsters darts around our heads. I grab my slingshot. Pa shakes his head at me and holds my arm back to tell me "no". For they are scared of us, coming to take their home. They finally find the clear sky and depart.

Dried bison jerky is handed around to quieten our murmuring tummies. The elders talk about our direction for tomorrow and my eyes start to close. Pa leads me to my sleep spot, where my reindeer mat is waiting, just far enough to allow the voices left by the fire to be softened by the walls but close enough to feel the warmth of the fire hold me. I reach in my bag for my little clay pot. Ma fills it with bear fat, adds a rolled piece of moss, borrows a flame from the fire to light it and nestles it into a thin ledge above me. My deer-skin blanket is laid on top of me. I love the way the fur tickles my face.

As Ma and Pa walk back to the fire, the flame from my tiny lamp makes their shadows as big as gentle giants sweeping across the walls, like a whisper of a story heard here before. Their stretched heads and bodies getting smaller as they glide back to the others at the fire, each body now casting its own shadow, making me feel safe within my tribe of flickering giants.

WHAT ABOUT WATER?

Our Stone Age ancestors relied on water for survival, just the same as we do. Water was needed to prevent dehydration, for cooking and to stay clean. It also meant plentiful food: fish, turtles, crayfish, water snails, reptiles, frogs, toads, alligators, even reeds and rushes.

Finding water

Our ancestors were pretty amazing at reading the land and understanding the clues that you or I may miss.

By reading the clouds, our ancestors would have known when it was going to rain and put out containers to collect water.

A scout sent on ahead from up high could have clearly seen dips and low points that indicate rivers.

Animals are likely to use the same trail to get to water, so following their tracks would have helped our ancestors find it too.

Water can extend a meal. One fish would not be enough food to feed a whole group, but fish soup might have been!

Hunter-gatherers were not always grubby and stinky. Cleaning and bathing would have meant a lower risk of illness.

Heating up water

How would early humans have heated water without pots or pans? They were very creative and would have used many different methods.

Animal hide

Hoisting a whole animal hide (skin) above the fire and lashing it onto a tripod of sticks created a natural container to boil water or cook stew. The fur would have singed off and the stew inside cooked nicely.

Clay pots

These would have been useful for cooking and boiling water nestled into the coals of a fire.

Hot-rock boiling

Containers made of birch bark or a hollowed-out wooden trough could be filled with water. Rocks (non-porous ones) were heated in the fire and added to the water, which would then gradually boil.

Natural springs bubbling up from underground would have been precious to find, offering fresh and safe drinking water.

Where to find natural springs may have been made part of storytelling, to make sure that the knowledge wasn't lost.

By listening carefully, our ancestors may have heard water trickling and followed the sound to find water.

Thirsty work

On average a human being can go without drinking water for three days. Next time you feel thirsty, spare a thought for our Stone Age ancestors who may have died in their quest to find a rare, secluded spring or river.

24 HOURS AS A HUNTER-GATHERER

Early hunter-gatherers were much like us in the way they went about their daily lives, only with a little more peril, general risk of death and a tad more wearing of dead animals. This is what may have happened to our Stone Age friend on a typical day.

6am: wake up

She awakens in the morning to the signal of the sun, instead of a hollering parent or an annoying alarm clock.

6.30am: wash

Time to get clean down at the river using a piece of wet leather to freshen up. Brushing teeth with a willow stick and a thin twig to pull out some meat from the night before works well.

7am: get dressed

Clothing comes from whatever is available. Today she wears a brain-tanned leather dress and some moose-skin rawhide sandals.

Clean your teeth Stone Age-style!

1 Find yourself a willow tree. Make sure you properly identify it first.
2 Gently break off a stick. Chew one end so that it looks a little like a paintbrush and use this to polish your teeth. You'll be surprised at how squeaky clean they feel.

7.30am: toilet time

When nature calls, she digs a small hole, listens to the birds to hear if they are signalling the presence of any dangerous lurking predators with their bird language, grabs a few soft mullein leaves for toilet paper and does what she needs to.

8am: time to eat

She eats when she is hungry, or when food is available. Today, the tribe will have dried berry cake with a dollop of bear fat. Later, she'll enjoy a few lightly toasted sweet chestnuts, plums from a nearby tree, some sweet and chewy pieces of bison jerky and a mushroom-and-roots stew.

9am-3pm: keep busy

She needs to check her fish traps down by the water's edge. Later, she will spend some time watching the bison nearby for clues on how best to ambush them. Then she will finish sharpening her fish hooks with sandstone and forage for some firewood.

3-5pm: rest and relax

Time for some creativity. She decides to add some cave art to the walls, using charcoal.

6.30pm: prepare for sleep

When the sun goes down, she stokes the fire, lights the fat lamps around the cave and prepares her bed. She sleeps inside a bison-skin sleeping bag, on top of a reindeer mat.

8.30pm: time to sleep

She snuggles down as her pa shares an epic hunting tale. As for lights out? Perhaps not... the more light there is, the more warmth and protection from predators, so leave them on!

STONE AGE FASHION

What people wore depended on the era and the climate they lived in. If it was hot, they may not have worn anything at all, or just a simple loin cloth. In colder climates (and if they were living in an era when sewing had been discovered), they would have worn as many layers as possible.

How were clothes made?

Early humans worked out how to turn animal skin into leather – a great material to make clothing from. The animal's brain was used to tan and soften the hide (skin), smoking it over a fire to preserve it.

Sewing needles were made using bone shards sharpened with stone. Fibres such as animal sinew (the fibre that connects muscle to bone) or gut string as well as thong made from leather scraps were used to sew the leather into clothes, bags and shoes.

For tough leather, holes would need to be punched first using a bone awl (an especially fat and sharp needle). Each piece of clothing could take a long time to make. But once made, they were strong and very long-lasting.

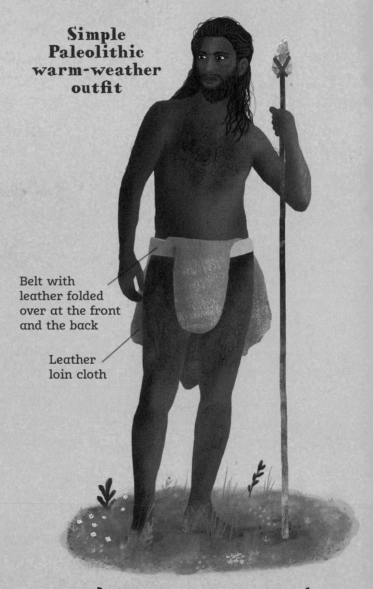

Simple Paleolithic warm-weather outfit

Belt with leather folded over at the front and the back

Leather loin cloth

How do we know?

It is impossible for us to know exactly what clothes looked like, as no complete garments exist today. However, archaeologists can build up ideas by looking at scientific evidence about the climate, tools, scraps of material and even the evolution of body lice!

Ivory beads, animal teeth and shells were used as jewellery and embellishments and as decoration for burials.

Warm-weather Mesolithic outfit

Shell beads

Brain-tanned tunic

Leather belt

Pouch for spare arrow tips, fish hooks and needles

Coconut shell cup

Elk-skin sandals with a rawhide sole

Cold-weather Mesolithic outfit

Wolverine fur trim

Horse-skin quiver

Giant beaver and deer-teeth necklace

Giant bison coat

Deer mittens

Sabre-tooth tiger leg bone knife in leather sheath

Dried grasses stuffed into boots for insulation

Brain-tanned boots

Accessories

Bearskin blanket

Straps made from mastodon leather

Irish elk antler button

Dire wolf tail

Other materials

Bark, grasses, rushes and reeds were used to create fabric. In the late Neolithic era, once animals were kept for farming, they had more access to wool to create new textiles, like felt.

23

HUNTING FOR FOOD

The land was like a hunter-gatherer's supermarket, but not all the food options gave up without a fight. Our ancestors had to make tools, work as a team and sometimes lose their lives hunting for food. Some techniques would have been riskier than others.

Animal traps

Traps were made from gut string, plant fibres, sticks, stones and bait. These would most likely have been to catch small game like rodents but bigger traps for wild boar or bear would have been set too.

Forests growing up quickly after the last ice age may have helped giant deer become extinct. Their giant antlers would have got stuck between the trees!

Hunting with weapons

Hunter-gatherers would have used sharpened sticks, hafted-stone spears, spear throwers (see box opposite), followed later by bows and arrows. They hunted alone and in groups for larger prey like giant deer and giant bison.

Bow and arrow

Flint arrowhead

Giant deer (Irish elk)

Now extinct, the giant deer, sometimes known as Irish elk (*Megaloceros giganteus*), roamed much of Eurasia until around the end of the last ice age. Some were taller than 7ft (2m) at the shoulders with enormous antlers. They would have been huge compared to a human standing next to them. Deer would have provided important nourishment, and much more, for our Stone Age ancestors (see page 30).

Antlers shed each spring would regrow by autumn

Antlers could be 12ft (4m) wide from tip to tip

Strong neck to support the huge antlers

Tracking and stalking

To hunt animals, our ancestors had to be sneaky, stealthy, crafty, cautious and really patient. From a young age, they would have learned how to watch for signs and clues that their prey was near. Sometimes they would have been lucky and may have been able to surprise a deer or other small animal but much would have been about careful planning.

Even when they had found an animal, they couldn't rush in. They would need to think about wind direction. Would the animal smell or hear them? Could they get a clean shot?

Animal signs

Looking for these signs can tell you if an animal has been nearby.

- Tracks on the ground
- Broken branches
- Compressed ground where the animal has slept
- Fur rubbed off on trees and prickly branches
- Fresh poo

Bear

Deer

Horse

Large cat

Ask a friend to stand blindfolded by a tree in the woods and try to creep up on them without them hearing you. See how hard it is? Each stick cracks, leaves crunch, even the grass makes a noise.

Spear thrower

This is an ancient weapon that was invented before the bow and arrow. It is a device that uses a flicking motion to give the spear more speed. The darts can travel up to 80mph (128kph). It works in a very similar way to the modern ball-launcher used by dog walkers.

Spear thrower

On some days they may have only had a small handful of bugs for dinner, on other days, a mammoth steak!

MAKE A BOW AND ARROW

Early hunter-gatherers would have carved their bows with flint knives and axes, used feathers for flights, flint and bone for arrow tips and used the fire to straighten their arrows with steam.

You will need

- **3 fresh hazel** or willow sticks about floor-to-chin height (one about 1in/2.5cm in diameter and two about ½in/1.25cm in diameter). They need to be fresh to get enough flexibility

- **Ball of string** or garden twine

- **Dowelling** or straight long sticks for arrows (fingertip to shoulder in length)

- **Duct tape** (about 4in/10cm)

- **Small piece of fabric** or leather (measure a circle using the bottom of a mug)

Remember, you are just practising, never aim or shoot at another living thing.

1 Tie the two thinner sticks together at both ends with string so that they are side by side. Top and tail them, so that one thick end is next to one thin end.

2 Tie the remaining stick on top of the other two sticks, securing with string at either end.

3 Wrap some more string around at the middle, about a hand's width, to create a handhold.

4 To make the bow string, tie a length of string on to either end of your bow so that it is tight.

5 Now for your arrow. Place the small round of fabric or leather centred onto one end of the dowelling or stick. Gather it around the tip and then tie it on around the stick to hold in place.

6 Stick the duct tape on the other end of the arrow with another piece over the top, making a sandwich with the stick in the middle. This will be the flight.

This type of arrow is called a 'blunt' and is used to stun birds in flight, preventing them from flying away injured and taking the precious arrow with them.

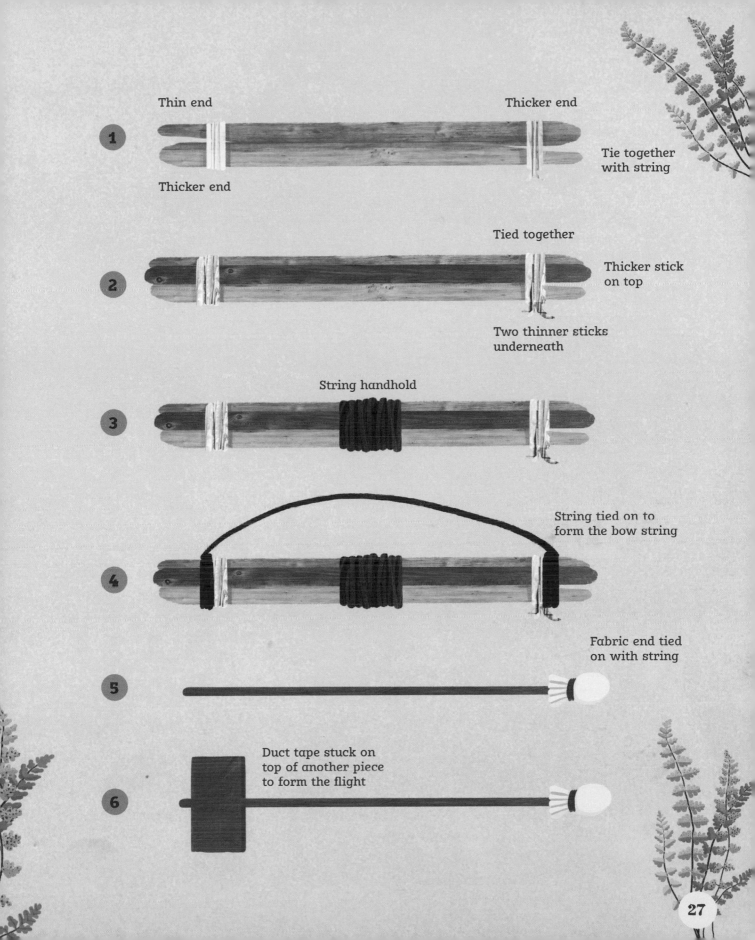

1 Thin end   Thicker end

Tie together with string

Thicker end

2 Tied together

Thicker stick on top

Two thinner sticks underneath

3 String handhold

4 String tied on to form the bow string

5 Fabric end tied on with string

6 Duct tape stuck on top of another piece to form the flight

PREPARING FOR THE HUNT

Pa has always told me amazing stories about hunting. I am eager to be strong and sure enough with my weapons to join in too. He talks about tracking, watching, stalking, waiting and then the ambush. The run, the chase, the shoot and then the blood trailing, thanksgiving, returning home with blood-stained clothes and wild stories. I make him tell me over and over again about the shot that made the kill. Who shot it? How far away were they? Did the arrow sing as it flew? I take up my bow and arrow, mimicking his every detail. He also reminds me of the hunters' rule that they never shoot an arrow if they do not believe they can kill, even if that means returning with no food. Each has their role, some scare the animals from the back, some make warning signals with bird calls laden with secret messages, but only a few are hunters to kill.

It's been a ritual, for as far back as I can recall the pictures in my head, that before a big hunt the tribe comes together with bows and arrows, spears and spear throwers for the weapon meet. This is where it is decided who the hunters will be. When I was three summers old, my ma gave me my first bow and arrow and now I can take part for the first time.

I watch as they take their places, lining up together, silently drawing back their bows, eyes focused. On my pa's call, they release their weapons towards the woven bundle of grasses and rushes. More take their place, a spear man, a younger girl and a man with eyes so black I call him flint-eyes. Shafts bound in rawhide, stone tips polished and perfected with careful blows from a rock, they take aim. Spear man takes a breath and releases. The girl closes her eyes, takes a deep breath, opens her eyes and releases the dart. I hear their arrows, darts and spears sing their freedom song as they glide through the air with speed and purpose, finding the target.

My turn now. I line up with the other young hunters, trying to quieten my heart and clear my mind just as I have been taught. I imitate the ways of the elders, gulping in air, focusing my breath. I pull back the bow string tight, my fingertips grazing my cheek. My fingers ache as my string digs in and urges me to let it ping free. I take a deep breath but I'm too excited, my fingers release the arrow too soon and it doesn't make the target this time. My body is rushing and tingling from the excitement. Pa says it was a fine shot and he praises me on my form.

At moonrise, as I climb into my bison-skin sleeping bag, I ask Pa to tell me more thrilling hunting stories. I'll dream of the hunt and be ready when it is time to take my place once again.

NOTHING WASTED

Our hunter-gatherer ancestors were respectful, resourceful and rarely wasted anything. When an animal was hunted and brought home to eat, they did not just see an opportunity for food – they made clothes, tools, jewellery, weapons, crafts and much more.

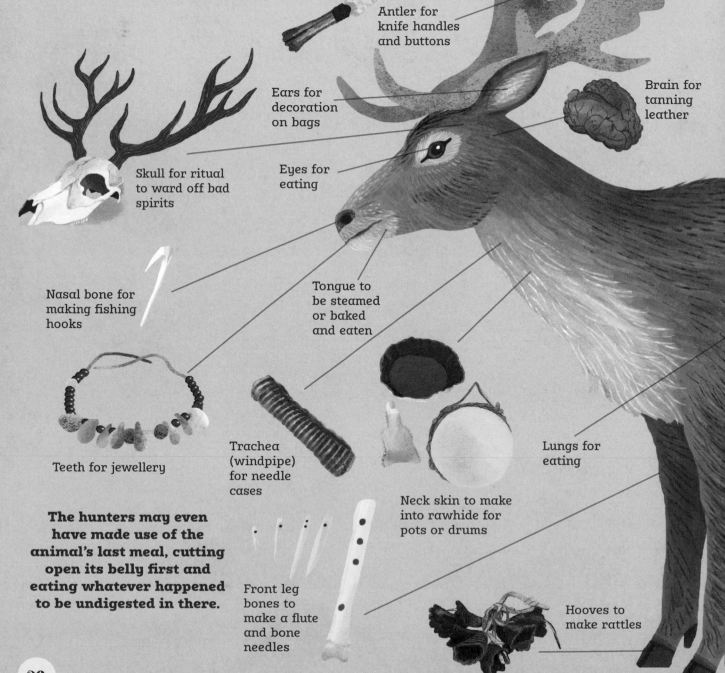

Antler for knife handles and buttons

Ears for decoration on bags

Brain for tanning leather

Skull for ritual to ward off bad spirits

Eyes for eating

Nasal bone for making fishing hooks

Tongue to be steamed or baked and eaten

Lungs for eating

Teeth for jewellery

Trachea (windpipe) for needle cases

Neck skin to make into rawhide for pots or drums

The hunters may even have made use of the animal's last meal, cutting open its belly first and eating whatever happened to be undigested in there.

Front leg bones to make a flute and bone needles

Hooves to make rattles

Back bones for making knives

Rib bones for scraping hides

Fat for eating and making medicines

Meat had to be prepared quickly to stop it from spoiling. Jerky would have been made to preserve the meat, cutting it into thin strips and smoking it over a fire.

Meat for eating and drying

Intestines for string and sewing fibres

Hide to make clothing

Tail for decoration

Dried poo used as a binder to make glue with pine resin

Sinew to be dried and pounded for thread

Stomach for tanning and making a bag

Guts for bait

Skin scraps to make hide glue

Bladder to make a water container

Blood used as a hardener to make clay floors and for drinking to replenish iron

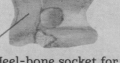

Heel-bone socket for bow-drill handle

KNOWING THE LAND

How did our Stone Age ancestors find their way around or make long journeys before GPS, compasses or maps were invented? By using nature as their guide, they could tell so much from the land, becoming better hunters and blending in with their surroundings.

Due to a lack of fur, human skin can draw attention with its shine. Using mud, chalk, clay, charcoal and natural paints they would have concealed their skin.

Creeping and stalking would be slow, but hunters would have been less likely to be noticed this way.

Shadow stick

On a bright sunny day, push a straight stick upright into flat ground. Put a stone where the tip of the shadow falls. This is the west point. Wait at least an hour. Mark the new point with another stone for the east point. Lay a stick matching up these two points. Get another stick, lay this to form a cross over the east/west points. This will give you north and south.

They may have rolled on the ground to pick up a more natural scent or used animal dung to disguise their smell.

Each animal footprint could be studied: Who left it? When were they there? What direction did they come from? Were they alone? Where were they going? Were they wounded?

Finding the North Star, 'Polaris', would have given a clear sign for finding north.

Our ancestors would have recognized where the Sun was at certain points in the day, using a shadow stick in the ground to help find its direction (see box opposite).

Looking at windswept trees and plants would have helped hunter-gatherers to understand about wind direction.

Small, fur-lined ears to reduce heat loss

4in (10cm) layer of fat under the skin for added insulation

Long tusks for digging up plants and fighting

Thick fur for extra warmth

They could grow as tall as 16ft (5m)

Ivory tusks were used to make beads, needles and even musical instruments

Woolly mammoth

These huge animals were found in many parts of the world during the last ice age and only became extinct about 10,000 years ago. They were an important source of food for early humans, living alongside each other for a few thousand years. Scientists know a lot about them because well-preserved mammoth remains have been found in the permafrost in Arctic regions.

FISHING TECHNIQUES

In modern times, we spend lots of money on expensive fishing kit: nets, hooks, bait, lines, reels and more. Early humans used simple kit sourced from nature and used carefully, with patience. They found many ways to feed themselves from the water, whether it was rivers, lakes or oceans.

Hook and line

Early humans made fishing lines from plant fibres and used bone and wood for fish hooks.

Fish traps

Willow traps made out of two interlocking long baskets would tempt a fish to swim in to get to some bait but not be able to get out again. This method relied on knowing where the fish were living and hiding.

Fishing nets

Nets made out of plant fibres could catch lots of fish in one go. They needed teamwork to get the net out and to pull it in again.

Spear fishing

This would have been done from boats or in shallow clear waters. Waiting... waiting... completely still... and then quickly taking the plunge when a fish was spotted. Someone using a spear thrower (see page 25) may have stood on a bank until they could take a shot.

Hunter-gatherers would have spent lots of time quietly watching the water and observing the fish before even trying to hunt them.

Fish tickling

In shallow waters trout like to hide between the rocks. By feeling in these crevices with hands, finding the belly, then hooking fingers in their gills they can be pulled out.

MAKE A GORGE HOOK

A gorge hook is an effective and simple tool that is still used today. Tied onto the end of a fishing line and baited with some juicy maggots or guts, the fish gulp down the bait, hook included, which then gets stuck in their mouths, lodging sideways. Hey presto, fish for dinner!

You will need

- **A twig** from any tree, about 1in (2.5cm) long
- **Whittling knife** or sharp piece of flint
- **Protective gloves**
- **Live bait** (a grasshopper is a great choice)
- **Fishing line**

Wear protective gloves and always cut in the direction away from yourself.

1 Sharpen the twig at either end using the knife or piece of flint. It needs to be pointed at both ends.

2 A shallow groove needs to be carved in the centre, creating a recess (or shallow indent) as this is where the fishing line will be tied and secured.

3 Tie your fishing line onto the hook, attach some live bait, lower into the water and then wait.

Fishing may have been a preferable method of hunting as fish tend not to bite your head off, like a fierce sabre-tooth tiger or charge you down like an angry mammoth!

FISH TAILS

I'm not quite old enough to go on a big hunt yet, but I always get to go on fishing trips. I even have my own line that I made from nettle and a hook that took me three moons to make. Best of all, I like hunting for the bait – grasshoppers! I catch sight of them jumping in the grass, with their springy legs, but I can jump higher.

It leaps, then I leap, surrounding it with my hands. Now in my grasp, I pinch its head off ready for the hook. It's funny how their legs still move around, as if they're trying to find their way home to tell about their adventures. But the fish like the wriggling, that's what attracts them.

We get to our fishing spot and sit quietly. I love watching Ma and the others as they tie their lines together with such fast fingers. I find a good stick and tie my line on. My fingers are slow but careful, especially when tying on the hook. My hook is my treasure. I bait a grasshopper and then wait. I know if I'm as still as a sleeping sloth then I may help to feed my tribe at moonrise. I can see the fish but they can't see me. The fish don't trust those who walk upright. I try to make sure my shadow isn't cast into the water, for she is a terrible hunter!

After a long wait, there is a bite! Just as I've seen the elders do, I fling my line behind me, where the fish is supposed to land and unhook. Its rainbow skin meets rock but it is still attached. Despairingly, my line tracks its force back towards the water. Its skin glints and flies through the air, over my head, back it goes, my hook now unattached sinking into the deepness. I grapple to grab it, slipping on the wet rocks, into the water. I see the rainbow-coloured fish swim swiftly off to tell tales of frightful dry land and two-legged beasts.

Ma laughs at my wet clothes and tells me I have much to learn. She is right. Ma and the others have caught many of the rainbow skins and reassures me that we'll eat well. I help prepare the fish, taking the insides out, saving them for bait. The bones are nestled into the coals. I love crunching into them. Pa likes the eyes best, he says they're juicy. I sneak some fishy flesh before it gets added to the mix of mushrooms, nuts and fat bubbling on the fire for later. I do not want to spend long eating, I want to start making a new fish hook. For a new sun will give me a fresh start to become a rainbow-skin hunter, just like my ma.

FORAGING

Hunter-gatherers walked the land, filling their bark baskets and rawhide containers with all the edible foods they could find. Some of these they would eat fresh, others they would take home to cook. They knew the land like we would know where to find things in the aisles of the supermarket.

Berries and fruits

These would have provided a sweet treat and a boost of energy. They may have enjoyed blackberries, elderberries, wild apples, wild strawberries and raspberries, drying some of them out in the sun to enjoy later.

Roots and tubers

Many plants that we call weeds, such as dandelion, cattails and burdock, would have provided precious energy from their roots.

Nuts and seeds

These would have been great snacks. Hazelnuts, sweet chestnuts and pine nuts could all have been enjoyed. Acorns would have been ground up to make flour but needed lots of processing and rinsing to make it edible.

Plants, bark and leaves

Lots of trees and plants produce edible leaves and flowers in the spring and summer. Autumn and winter would have provided limited fresh food. Our ancestors may have eaten inner cedar bark or lichens at these times.

Mushrooms

They could have eaten various types of fungi during the winter months by drying them out and adding them to stews.

The amount of energy it took to forage for food was important so that they didn't burn more calories trying to gather it than the food actually provided.

MAKE A DIGGING STICK

These would have been used to dig around plants more easily and with less risk of damaging the stem or breaking the root.

You will need

- **A thick stick** about 2–3ft (60–90cm) long and about 2in (5cm) in diameter

- **Charcoal** or natural paints for decorating

- **An abrasive rock** small enough to use as a tool

1 Peel the bark off the stick. Use the rock to make one end of the stick sharp and pointed.

2 You can decorate it with charcoal or natural paints. Our ancestors may have used fire to make creative markings.

Archaeologists have found fragments of ancient digging sticks all over the world and some indigenous peoples still use them today for practical tasks and in ceremonies.

Edible bugs

Bugs would have made a delicious bite-sized meal! Some gooey, juicy grubs could be eaten raw. Maggots on rotting meat could have been a feast and perhaps grasshoppers, enjoyed toasted gently over the fire on a stick, like a kebab.
Yum yum?

STONE AGE RECIPES

Would you like to experience some of the tastes and smells that may have been very familiar to a Stone Age hunter-gatherer? Have a go at making some of these delicious recipes and they may become your new snack-time favourites.

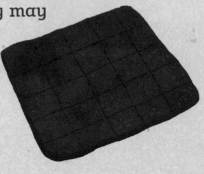

Pemmican

Pemmican is a perfect high-energy snack and is still enjoyed today. Anything that has stood the test of that much time must be good! It is best enjoyed while out hiking.

Ingredients

You will need a ratio of 1:1 of the dry ingredients and the wet fat

- Fat (goose fat or lard)
- Dried jerky (beef or venison)
- Dried berries (cranberries or blueberries work really well)
- Nuts (optional)

1 Blend up the meat jerky in a food processor or grind it by hand using a pestle and mortar. Blend up the dried berries. You can blend these into a powder or leave them a bit chunkier, depending on if you want a rougher texture with some little flavour bombs popping up. If you want to add some nuts, blend those up now too. Mix all the dry ingredients together in a bowl.

2 Melt the fat in a saucepan and let it cool down. Mix the melted fat and the dried ingredients, stirring together well. Pour out your mixture onto a large baking sheet, covering it completely. Put it in the fridge to cool and harden.

3 Leave it overnight, then take out and cut it up into squares. Keep it in an airtight container.

It probably isn't true that Stone Age people ate bland and dull food. Evidence has been found in ancient clay pots of seeds, such as garlic mustard (*Alliaria petiolata*), being used for spice.

Nettle-seed bread balls

Nettle seeds offer valuable fats and vitamins, so the sting would have been an easy trade-off for our ancestors. Flour would have been made by grinding up various nuts and seeds.

Ingredients

- 3½oz (100g) any type of flour
- About 4 tbsp water
- 1 tbsp nettle seeds
- Sprinkle of garlic granules
- Salt and pepper

1 Mix the nettle seeds, salt, pepper and flour in a bowl.

2 Keep adding small amounts of water until the dough holds together nicely but isn't sticky.

3 Roll the dough into small balls using your hands, place them onto a baking tray and cook in the oven on 350°F (180°C/gas mark 4) for about 12–15 minutes. They are ready when they are brown all over.

Harvesting nettle seeds

Wearing gloves, pick several nettle stems with the seeds still attached. With a piece of paper underneath and your gloved hands, roll and rub the seeds and watch them fall onto the paper.

Hunter-gatherer tea

Make a warming and medicinal tea. You can use whatever plants or herbs you like, as long as you are totally sure what they are and that they are safe to consume.

Ingredients

For a delicious combination, try a handful each of:

- Mint leaves
- Nettle leaves (use gloves)
- Spruce needles*

1 Cover the herbs and plants with water in a small saucepan.

2 Bring to a gentle boil.

3 Strain through a sieve and enjoy, once cooled down.

*Make sure you check which needles you are using and are totally sure what they are. Do not mix up spruce and yew (*Taxus baccata*), which is very toxic.

HOW MANY WAYS CAN YOU USE A STONE?

Early humans used stone, like flint and obsidian, to make the first ever tools known to man, such as knives, arrowheads and spears. But stone wasn't only used to make tools and weapons – it was used for many other daily tasks. How many different ways can you think of to use a stone?

- As a grinding tool
- Sanding and shaping wood
- Chipping away at (and with) to create stone sculptures
- Weighing down fish traps and nets
- Making small traps
- Making holes in leather for clothing
- Digging tools
- Building stone circles and sacred monuments
- A canvas for cave art
- Banging together to make music
- Shaping to make beads and buttons
- To make sparks for fire
- In games
- To create a hearth for a fireplace

- Heating water
- Warming up and wrapping in leather for a cold night
- Cooking food on, like a frying pan
- Surrounding an underground cooking pit
- Building houses and shelters
- Knife blade for cutting meat and killing prey
- Hammer stone to shape other stone into tools
- As a hand axe
- Spear, arrow or dart head
- For throwing at prey
- As a scraper

Flint

Obsidian

Sandstone

Hard rock

Stonehenge

Stonehenge is one of the world's most famous ancient monuments, found in Wiltshire, UK. Experts believe it was built in late Neolithic times but they still don't know exactly how or even why. Some people think it was used as a place to hold special ceremonies and celebrate sacred moments in the seasons.

MAKE AN ARROWHEAD (OR SPEAR HEAD)

These days most of us don't have to hunt in order to survive, but it's still fun to have a go at an ancient skill. Today, many of the tools we use could make this job much quicker but, back then, it could have taken days to perfect.

You will need

- **Small piece of slate** no bigger than the size of a slice of bread

- **Pencil**

- **Flat, hard rock** larger than your slate

- **Hammering stone** (this is a round stone, heavier than your slate)

- **Piece of sandstone** or abrasive rock (an old brick also works)

1 Draw a triangle shape onto the piece of slate, the size you wish your arrowhead to be.

2 Place the slate on top of the flat rock, with the bits you don't want hanging off the edge. Use the hammering stone to gently begin tapping around the shape, breaking bits off to create the right shape. You should now have a rough arrow shape.

3 Now use the piece of sandstone to rub over the arrowhead backwards and forwards until you have smooth edges and a sharp point.

You could lash the arrowhead onto a stick with string, or glue it. Did you know that Stone Age people used a mix of pine resin, ground-up egg shells and animal poo to make their own glue?

PLANT MEDICINE

Our ancestors would have faced constant dangers – animal attacks, cuts from tools, the occasional slip off a cliff while chasing a mammoth, and more! With no hospitals or doctors' surgeries, they had to rely on nature's medicine cabinet and the precious knowledge of the healers in their tribe.

If you are not 100% sure about a plant, do NOT pick it. Only pick from safe areas away from heavy traffic and dog walking. Only take what you need and ask the landowner's permission first.

Yarrow (*Achillea millefolium*)
Can help stop bleeding by packing it into a wound.

Comfrey (*Symphytum officinale*)
Can help heal broken bones and soothe bruises.

Try making some warming hunter-gatherer tea from dandelion flowers, leaves or roots and rosemary leaves, see page 41.

Dandelion (*Taraxacum*)
Gets rid of toxins in the body and is high in vitamin C.

Rosemary (*Salvia rosmarinus*)
Can help to kill harmful bacteria.

Bark
Stiff bark, held on with plant fibres and tree roots, may have been used to help keep broken bones still, like a primitive plaster cast.

Moss
Some mosses work well as a cold compress to soothe bumps and sprains.

The average lifespan of a Stone Age person was 35 years.

Birch polypore mushroom (*Piptoporus betulinus*)
Slices may have been used as plasters. They have healing properties too, like helping to kill harmful bacteria.

Acorns
These have astringent and antiseptic properties and can be used to treat diarrhoea, pain, swelling and even for drawing out splinters.

Make your own soothing compress

Plantain is a common weed that can be found in back gardens, parks, along the edges of roads and footpaths. Next time you are stung by a stinging nettle or an angry wasp, find some plantain leaves. Make them moist, either by putting them in your mouth and chewing up a little, or by dabbing some water on them. Press onto your wound for around five minutes and you'll be surprised at how quickly the sting is relieved!

Broadleaf plantain (*Plantago major*)
Great for relieving bites, stings and burns.

NOT ALL WORK, WORK, WORK!

Early humans were probably only truly active for two or three hours each day. They had to save energy as they never knew when they might need to chase or run! Although there would have been many chores, other times would have been spent doing more meaningful or fun things.

Music

You might think of music as a modern-day invention, but it is actually an ancient pastime. Drums were made from animal skin and wood, rattles made from animal hooves, whistles made from leg bones and flutes made from wood. Even stones and sticks being banged together would have created a fantastic beat around the fire.

A conch shell found in a cave in southern France is thought to be the oldest known wind instrument at 17,000 years old.

Socializing

Stone Age people did not always spend time in small groups. It is believed that occasionally different tribes would meet, creating larger gatherings. They may have used this time to trade goods and come together for celebrations.

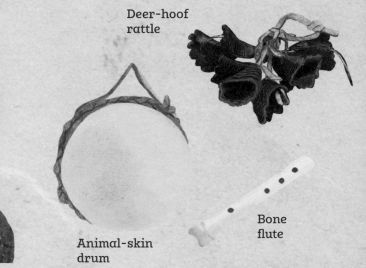

Deer-hoof rattle

Animal-skin drum

Bone flute

Rituals

Deaths would have been marked, hunts and big kills celebrated, and the Earth's elements and wild creatures worshipped, through dance, cave art, music and fire. Sometimes the dead were buried with tools, food and jewellery, if they were someone who carried importance within the tribe, like a shaman (someone who looked after the health and spiritual well-being of the group).

Remains of highly decorated people have been found at the Paleolithic burial site at Sunghir, in Russia.

Art

Our early ancestors painted on cave walls, often showing human hands, abstract patterns and large animals. Archaeologists have also found remains of clay and stone figurines carved or chipped out with fine details.

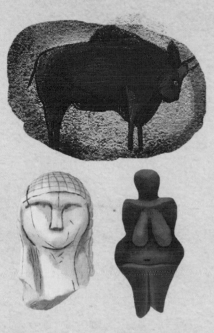

Ancient cave art has been found on every continent, except Antarctica.

The oldest known cave painting, of a wild pig, was found in Indonesia and is thought to be around 45,000 years old.

Play

Playing hide and seek would have helped develop camouflage and stalking techniques. Fun with bows and arrows would have been great target practice and any games involving running would have been good training.

The seasons

Our ancestors moved with the seasons, lived their lives in tune with them and celebrated the changes. For example, the winter solstice is the day of the year with the fewest hours of daylight. After the winter solstice, days start becoming longer and nights shorter as spring approaches. They may have visited ancient sites such as Stonehenge (see page 42) for this sort of celebration.

CELEBRATING THE HUNT

I hear the hunters returning before I see them. Their howls and yowls pull me from my sleeping moon-time visions. I race to see them coming over the hill. One at the front with a stick balanced on his shoulder, blood covering his clothes, and one taking the weight from the back. A fine buck, threaded on, his legs bound with vines. His antlers must make up half the heaviness.

The elders set upon him with their sharp stone tools and his meat is wrapped in the hide to stop the dirt getting in. Pa and the others have a pit dug out of the earth, which is already being heated with rocks lining the bottom and sides. By the time the moon comes out we will be gorging on deer like animals. I gather the giant leaves and wrap the meat up ready for the pit. We all help put the earth back on, patting it down with our feet, giving thanks to the land for all it offers us.

It feels like many suns have passed before we can uncover our hidden feast, but it is only one. The soil is warm under my hands, like the land is erupting with anticipation, just like my tummy! The deeper we dig, the hotter it gets. The moon's light guides us and our mammoth-sized fire illuminates the unveiling, ready to celebrate. The gigantic bundle of leaves is hefted out, falling open like a gift to offer us the steaming meat. Ma and some others play their rawhide drums loudly in gratitude.

As our bundle cools, our bodies stir to the growing rhythm. I shake my head so that my hair whips my face, my mouth allowing new sounds to join the celebration. Others bang sticks against the cave walls and rocks together to make echoes through the air. Some of the elders gather charcoal and ochres to speak of the hunt in pictures, drawing out the lines in the rock to show us the story in detail, grabbing a bark torch so that the pictures move and flow with shadows and light.

I take some charcoal in my mouth, using my teeth to grind it up, my nose scrunching at each crunch, and then I place my hand onto the rocks and blow out the paint from my mouth, leaving the memory of my hand behind. And then, Pa stands and the rhythm stands still. The ground bugs and the beasts of the sky offer the only sound. His words bring us back to now, to thank the deer for allowing us to be here for another sun.

After his words, we all dig in. I grab a bone and suck out the nectar from the inside. I love it when it's still warm. I pull handfuls of flesh from where it falls from the bone and wolf it down. I take one more handful and lay next to the fire, watching the tiny dancing fires fly above my head, letting the juice dribble down my chin. The drumming starts again and more of my tribe begin to move their bodies, circling the fire. But I close my eyes, grateful for our feast, and let all the noises in my ears mix with the happy feelings in my body and the fullness of my tummy.

MAKE YOUR OWN CAVE ART

We can't ask our ancestors why they painted on cave walls but we can try to imagine. Perhaps they used their art to communicate and tell stories? Maybe it was to pass the time? Or maybe just because they were beautiful. Here are a few ideas of how to create your own art.

Spraying with charcoal

Ask an adult before you do this! Chew up a piece of cold charcoal. This is quite a disgusting thing to do! Crunch it up but do NOT swallow. Let the moisture in your mouth make it a bit wet. If you need to, take a tiny sip of water. Keep crunching until it is really fine. Place your hand on a rock wall or piece of slate (or card or fabric), purse your lips and spit out little bits all over your hand. Keep going until your hand is covered. Remove your hand slowly, revealing the outline.

Archaeologists think that the hands in the Cueva de las Manos in Argentina were made using a spray pipe made of bone. Maybe this was like a type of Stone Age signature?

The Chauvet caves

Some of the earliest known cave paintings in Europe were found in the Chauvet caves in France, dating back to around 37,000 years ago. Some of the paintings are stencils of handprints, others just dots. But some show lifelike animals like cave bears, bison, horses, aurochs, giant deer, musk ox, and panthers all galloping, crawling, frolicking, flying and in some, fighting and battling.

On slate or stone

Find a large piece of slate. This is your 'cave wall' canvas. Use charcoals and chalks to draw an animal you might imagine roamed during the Stone Age. The best part is that you can rub it off and start again as many times as you like!

Draw a nature story

Using a piece of card, a portion of an old sheet or other fabric, imagine an epic hunting battle. Draw your story using only natural materials found outside to create colour and movement. Try using berries, rubbing on grasses and using charcoal for shading.

Stone Age people used beautiful natural ochres (colourful pigments in the rocks) charcoal, chalks, berries, blood and sometimes even poo! They used their fingers and their mouths to leave the marks.

Feather paintbrush

Find a small stick with an inner pith. Elder (*Sambucus nigra*) works well. Find a small feather and cut off an end. Sink it into the end of the stick, through the middle. Now you have a natural paintbrush. You can also try this with pine needles or tiny sticks and see the different markings they make.

Get a different view

Try creating your artwork by attaching a sheet of paper or fabric with adhesive tape onto a wall or the underside of a table. Feel what it was like to draw on a cave wall. Try turning off the lights too and use a dim torch to get a real feel for painting in a darkened cave.

COULD YOU HAVE SURVIVED THE STONE AGE?

Living in the Stone Age was a constant battle for survival. Where would your next meal come from? Was your next meal also coming to eat you too? Where would you sleep and keep warm? All of these things would have been on your mind daily. Think about the questions here and talk about your answers with a friend, parent, carer or teacher.

1 Our Stone Age ancestors were very inventive. Often one tool would do three or four different jobs, if not more. Think about the list below and how many different ways each item could be used. Be creative!

- **Smooth large rock**
- **Piece of flint**
- **Leg bone**
- **Animal hide**
- **Ball of clay**
- **Stick**
- **Grass**

2 Our ancestors had to travel light. Think about a normal day in your modern world. Think about everything you use on a daily basis that enables you to survive and live comfortably. Now, from these items, you may only choose four to keep with you. What would they be and why? Remember, if you decide to keep a TV, what about electricity? If you decide to choose food, how would you cook it?

3 Early humans needed many skills in order to be able to survive and thrive – like archery, plant identification, weaving, pottery, trap making and many more. Can you think of any more skills you might have needed to be able to survive? What skills do you think you have, today, that could help you or a group survive?

4 Sometimes our ancestors lived in groups, which meant more mouths to feed but plenty of people to lend a hand. Sometimes they lived on their own, so there was only one mouth to feed but only one person to look out for food and do all the jobs that needed to get done. Do you think you would be better at taking care of just yourself or living in a community?

5 What raw materials do you think you might need to make your own tools, clothing and shelter? Think about the details. What might you use for glue to stick stone to wood for handles? What would you use to stitch your clothing?

6 What type of tool or weapon would you choose to take on a hunt with you? What type of Stone Age animal would you least like to face?

7 Which period of the Stone Age would most suit you? Which of the following would you rather be?

a) Paleolithic scavenger: wild, scavenging for food, discovering fire, enduring ice ages and living in caves.

b) Mesolithic traveller: moving with the seasons, getting to know where the good food travels or grows, seeing lots of new places and starting to live with people in small tribes.

c) Neolithic farmer: living in communities, lots more mouths to feed and people to look after, many more skills learned, farming lifestyle, people starting to domesticate animals and food growing next to houses.

GLOSSARY

aurochs
An extinct species of horned wild cattle. One of the largest herbivores in Europe after the last ice age.

blunt arrow
A 'blunt' was an arrow without a sharp point used to hunt birds. The idea was to stun them and then kill them, rather than try to hunt them in mid-flight and risk injuring them without a kill.

daub
A type of mud plaster made from a combination of clay, straw, soil and animal dung. Used to cover homes, becoming a hard insulated wall or roof.

evolution
The change in characteristics of a species over a number of generations, relying on the process of natural selection.

extinction
If a plant or animal species becomes extinct, it means that no individual lives anywhere in the world. That species has died out.

fish tickling
The process of fishing by hand, using the crevices of the rocks and riverbanks where the fish hide. Trapping the fish against the sides and putting fingers into its gills.

fish trap
A woven double-funnelled basket to catch fish. The fish go in to get the bait and get stuck in between the baskets, making it nearly impossible to escape.

flint
A very hard black or grey rock used to make sparks for fire, or for making tools like arrows and knives. Well known for its very sharp edges.

flint knapping
The art of breaking sections off a piece of flint using a hard stone.

giant deer (or Irish elk)
A huge, extinct species of deer.

gill net
A large fishing net made up of many knots used to catch fish in large quantities.

hafting
The process of attaching a handle or strap to an artefact such as bone or stone.

hide (animal)
The skin of a large animal. Taken from the German word 'haut', which means skin.

hominid
The group consisting of all humans and great apes, including both modern and extinct species.

Homo erectus
The first of our ancient relatives to have human-like body size and shape. It was also the first known of the early human species to migrate out of Africa. The name translates to 'upright man'.

Homo ergaster
One of our ancient ancestors. Its name translates to 'work man' or 'skilled man'.

Homo habilis
An early ancestor whose name translates to 'handy man', based on their stone tool-making abilities.

Homo sapiens
This is the name given to our modern human species. Our name translates to 'wise man'.

hunter-gatherer
These people search, forage and hunt for their food.

ice age
Long periods of time where the Earth's temperature dropped, causing large areas to be covered in snow and ice glaciers. The last ice age ended about 11,700 years ago.

jerky
Dried strips of meat.

mastodon
A relation to the mammoth, but shorter and stockier.

megafauna
Very large animals, which can be extinct or living today.

Mesolithic
The middle portion of the Stone Age.

Neanderthal
An extinct species of hominid. A distant cousin of *Homo sapiens*. They existed thousands of years before our modern species but became extinct due to a smaller population.

Neolithic
The 'new age' of the Stone Age, introducing the start of living in settlements and farming.

obsidian
A volcanic rock formed by the rapid cooling of lava. Used to make extremely sharp tools.

Paleolithic
The start of the Stone Age, spanning over three million years.

pemmican
A Stone Age staple food made by compressing dried meat, berries, nuts and fats for an 'on the go', calorie-rich snack.

sabre-tooth tiger
An extinct species of cat, characterized by their long, curved, sharp front teeth.

spear thrower
An ancient throwing device that pre-dates the bow and arrow. It propels a spear or dart at great speed.

tanning
The process of turning animal skins and hides into leather. Usually using the brain of the animal to soften the skin and smoking over a fire to preserve the leather.

tinder
Dry materials used to catch a spark when starting a fire.

wolverine
A powerful stocky animal that resembles a small bear. However, it is not a bear but part of the weasel family.

woolly mammoth
A gigantic extinct species, closely related to the elephant, with long trunk, giant tusks and covered in long hair.

55

ABOUT THE AUTHOR

Naomi Walmsley runs Outback2Basics with her partner Dan, from their patch of woodland in Shropshire, UK. Specializing in bushcraft and Stone Age skills, they provide unique experiences for schoolchildren and teachers to connect with nature. Naomi is also a qualified bushcraft and Forest School instructor. So passionate is she about the Stone-Age way of life, she has actually lived and breathed it for herself. With Dan, she undertook a five-month Stone-Age immersion experience in the US, living in the wilderness without any modern equipment. They also appeared in Channel 4's fascinating *Surviving the Stone Age* documentary – a three-part series filmed in Bulgaria with six other Stone-Age experts, living as a tribe of hunter-gatherers for one month. Naomi has co-authored two previous books for GMC Publications, *Forest School Adventure* and *Urban Forest School*. She has also written for many magazines, including *Bushcraft & Survival Skills*, *Living Woods* and *Juno*.

www.outback2basics.co.uk
Instagram and Twitter: @outback2basics

Acknowledgements

Thanks to Dr Theresa Emmerich Kamper for her expert knowledge and help.

First published 2022 by Button Books, an imprint of Guild of Master Craftsman Publications Ltd, Castle Place, 166 High Street, Lewes, East Sussex, BN7 1XU, UK. Copyright in the Work © GMC Publications Ltd, 2022. ISBN 978 1 78708 120 8. Distributed by Publishers Group West in the United States. All rights reserved. The right of Naomi Walmsley to be identified as the author of this work has been asserted in accordance with the Copyright, Designs and Patents Act 1988, sections 77 and 78. No part of this publication may be reproduced, stored in a retrieval system, or transmitted in any form or by any means without the prior permission of the publisher and copyright owner. While every effort has been made to obtain permission from the copyright holders for all material used in this book, the publishers will be pleased to hear from anyone who has not been appropriately acknowledged and to make the correction in future reprints. The publishers and author can accept no legal responsibility for any consequences arising from the application of information, advice, or instructions given in this publication. A catalogue record for this book is available from the British Library. Publisher: Jonathan Bailey, Production: Jim Bulley, Jon Hoag, Senior Project Editor: Virginia Brehaut, Designer: Robin Shields, Illustrator: Mia Underwood. Colour origination by GMC Reprographics. Printed and bound in China.

FSC
www.fsc.org
MIX
Paper from responsible sources
FSC® C016973

Button Books

For more on Button Books, contact:
GMC Publications Ltd, Castle Place,
166 High Street, Lewes, East Sussex,
BN7 1XU, United Kingdom
Tel: +44 (0)1273 488005
buttonbooks.co.uk/buttonbooks.us